THE FLAG WITH FIFTY-SIX STARS

A Gift from the Survivors of Mauthausen

by Susan Goldman Rubin

illustrated by Bill Farnsworth

Holiday House / New York

The Mauthausen flag reproduced on pages 34–35
is courtesy of the Simon Wiesenthal Center Library and Archives, Los Angeles, California.

Library of Congress Cataloging-in-Publication Data
Rubin, Susan Goldman.
The flag with fifty-six stars: a gift from the survivors of Mauthausen /
by Susan Goldman Rubin ; illustrated by Bill Farnsworth.— 1st ed.
p. cm.
Includes bibliographical references and index.
ISBN 0-8234-1653-4 (hardcover)
ISBN 0-8234-2019-1 (paperback)
1. Mauthausen (Concentration camp)—Juvenile literature.
2. World War, 1939–1945—Concentration camps—
Liberation—Germany—Juvenile literature.
3. Flags—United States—Juvenile literature.
I. Farnsworth, Bill. II. Title.
D805.5.M38R83 2005
940.53'18362—dc22
2004047457

ISBN-13: 978-0-8234-1653-0 (hardcover)
ISBN-13: 978-0-8234-2019-3 (paperback)

ISBN-10: 0-8234-1653-4 (hardcover)
ISBN-10: 0-8234-2019-1 (paperback)

ACKNOWLEDGMENTS

Many people helped me with this book. First, I want to thank Adaire J. Klein, director of Library and Archival Services; Fama Mor, former archivist and curator; Leah Angell Sievers, manager of museum educational programs; and the rest of the Library and Archival Services staff of the Simon Wiesenthal Center Museum of Tolerance.

I thank Simon Wiesenthal for corresponding with me and giving me permission to quote from his 1980 U.S. Congressional Medal of Honor acceptance speech.

I am grateful to Peter Seibel, who reminisced about his father. I also thank Dr. Přemysl Dobiáš; Bill Drake; and Professor David Wingeate Pike, an authority on Mauthausen who teaches at the University of Paris.

A letter from Chaplain Mark A. Geeslin in the archives at the Simon Wiesenthal Center led me to Ralph Storm and Engineer Historian Raymond S. Buch. These men of the 11th Armored Division who liberated Mauthausen generously shared their recollections with me and forwarded issues of *The Thunderbolt*. Ray Buch also sent me videotapes that included movies and photographs that he and other men of the 11th Armored Division took at Mauthausen in May 1945. Chaplain Geeslin, who became a judge after the war, put me in touch with Mike Jacobs, a survivor of Mauthausen and one of the founders of the Dallas Memorial Center for Holocaust Studies. All of these eyewitnesses assured me that they wanted this story of the liberation of the concentration camp at Mauthausen told to children.

I also want to thank my editor, Mary Cash, for not only believing in this book, but for discovering vital information that enlarged our understanding of historic events. As always, I owe a debt of thanks to my agent, George Nicholson, for his endless enthusiasm. And finally, I want to express gratitude to my husband, Michael, for his support.

During the dark days of the Holocaust, the Nazis built their last concentration camp: Mauthausen.

Heinrich Himmler, head of the SS (*Schutzstaffel*), an elite division of the Nazi Party, picked the location himself. Set high on a hill overlooking the Danube River in Austria, Mauthausen had once been a popular hiking area. But Himmler chose the spot for its granite quarries. The quarries provided stones for paving city streets—and for constructing buildings in nearby Linz, the hometown of Adolf Hitler, leader of the Nazi Party. The camp would house the slave labor the Nazis would use to mine the granite.

Hitler had selected Himmler as chief of the SS in 1929. Before then, Himmler had raised chickens on a farm near Munich, Germany. Once he proved his ruthlessness and fanatical devotion to Hitler, he became one of the most powerful men in the Nazi Party.

Beginning in 1938, Himmler's men arrested people who opposed Hitler and the Nazis, shipping them to Mauthausen. Among the first prisoners to arrive were Spaniards, who constructed barracks surrounded by electrified barbed wire fences and high stone walls. A carved German eagle mounted on top of a huge wooden gate loomed over new arrivals.

When World War II broke out in September 1939, Himmler's SS police arrested thousands of men, women, and children in the countries that Germany conquered. Some of those arrested were spies and secret agents. Others simply belonged to groups Himmler and Hitler hated—Gypsies (often called the Roma people), Jehovah's Witnesses, homosexuals, and Jews. They all suffered under inhumane conditions.

Prisoners had to wear colored triangles sewn to their uniforms indicating their "crimes" in the eyes of the Nazis. For example, brown was for Gypsies, pink for homosexuals, purple for Jehovah's Witnesses, and yellow for Jews.

Brutal *Kapos,* who were prisoners appointed by the Nazis, supervised the slaves in the quarries while the SS looked on. Women and men, including strong boys over twelve, hauled heavy stones up 186 steps. Those who paused to rest or tried to escape were executed. A band of musicians would accompany them to the gallows.

Himmler kept Mauthausen a secret from the world. No one was to tell about it, not even townspeople who passed the quarries and saw the prisoners. If anybody disobeyed, the penalty was death.

"Everyone was afraid," recalled Frau Juan S., a woman from the village of Mauthausen who was later interviewed by author Gordon Horwitz.

As the war raged on, Himmler opened a new subcamp called Gusen I a few miles away from Mauthausen. He ranked Mauthausen and Gusen I as Grade III camps: the worst. No one would return from them alive, he said.

Many inmates gave up hope. But others, such as Mike Jacobs, a Jewish teenager from Poland, believed they would survive Mauthausen. "I never gave up my belief," said Jacobs. "Dreaming of freedom is really what kept me going. In my mind I was still a free person."

By September 1941, Germany, along with fellow Axis countries Italy and Japan, was at war with nearly all of Europe, the Allied forces. The Nazis stepped up production of weapons. Himmler's SS ordered inmates to carve out enormous tunnels in the hills behind Gusen I. As the tunnels were finished, the Nazis set up subterranean factories, hidden from view of enemy planes.

When the United States entered the war in December 1941 and joined the Allies, Himmler opened more and more subcamps, such as Gusen II and Gusen III—until there were approximately sixty in all.

Mike Jacobs worked in the tunnels of Gusen II. His job was to make aluminum parts for the jet fighters flown by the German air force. However, Mike joined an underground movement and sabotaged the planes by purposely connecting the parts in the wrong places. "I had such a good feeling," he remembered. "We were the ones causing the planes to crash. In a way, we were helping the Allies win the war."

In 1944, Allied troops began turning the tide against the Axis forces. They advanced toward Austria and Germany. As they drew closer and closer to the concentration camps, Himmler realized he would need to hide his crimes. He gave new orders. "No prisoner is to fall alive into enemy hands," he declared. So he evacuated prisoners from concentration camps in Poland, Czechoslovakia, and other countries and transported them to Mauthausen.

During the winter of 1944 and the first months of 1945, tens of thousands of prisoners arrived at Mauthausen and its subcamps. Those too sick to work huddled together in huts and tents. With every trainload of new arrivals, food became ever scarcer. Starving prisoners ate leaves, grass, even pieces of coal.

"The hunger was almost unbearable," wrote Simon Wiesenthal, a Jewish architect from Poland who had been imprisoned for four years. "I had virtually given up all hope of staying alive."

But during the spring of 1945, the Nazis realized they would definitely lose the war. British and American troops were approaching from the west, Soviet troops from the east. Rumors spread that the war would end soon. Many prisoners wondered if they would live to see it.

Wiesenthal and his fellow inmates heard the sound of American planes overhead. "One day we saw an air battle taking place before our very eyes," recalled Zvi Barlev, a Jewish teenager from Poland.

Another time the Nazis hit a U.S. Navy espionage plane. Lieutenant Jack H. Taylor, a special agent who had grown up in California, bailed out in his parachute. The SS captured Taylor and held him at Mauthausen.

Nevertheless, the sound of planes brought hope. Would the Americans get there in time, though? The prisoners all prayed that they could hold out long enough. With only one bowl of watery soup to eat each day, it would not be easy.

In April 1945, Allied forces invaded Austria. Prisoners who worked in the homes of the SS guards overheard radio broadcasts. Members of the underground had foraged for parts and assembled their own radio receivers. Přem Dobiáš, a lawyer from Czechoslovakia who had been imprisoned at Mauthausen for three years, secretly listened to the news on his handmade radio set.

On May 3, most of the SS guards ran away before they could be captured by Allied troops. Firemen and police officers from Vienna who were Nazi sympathizers arrived and took charge.

On May 4, everyone in the camp knew that the Americans were nearby. Perhaps they'd reach Mauthausen that very night! In preparation, Lieutenant Taylor taught the band of musicians how to play "The Star-Spangled Banner."

Now that freedom seemed close at hand, other prisoners felt inspired to make something that symbolized their faith in the future. With what little strength they had, they began a secret project.

Hastily, they scrounged around the camp for materials. First, they swiped coarse sheets from the SS laundry. They took red from Nazi banners that prisoners had ripped down in the village of Mauthausen and smuggled in. Bluish gray fabric came from prisoners' ragged jackets. They found needles and thread belonging to their former block commanders. A workshop where prisoners had made uniforms for the Nazis provided a sewing machine.

The prisoners worked quickly as they waited for the Americans. Their fingers trembled with excitement. Sewing helped them forget their hunger. With rows of tiny, even stitches, they attached strips of red to the wrinkled sheet, forming stripes. They cut star shapes out of the faded blue cloth. Then they stitched the edges to hold the piece in place. The off-white sheet underneath showed through the star cutouts. At night, when it was too dark to see, they rolled up their surprise and hid it under the floorboards.

Meanwhile, Himmler had been worrying about what would happen to him when the Allies arrived in Mauthausen. He made an outrageous plan. He would put all the inmates of Gusen I and Gusen II into the tunnels, along with the local villagers. Then he would seal the entrance and blow up everyone. Himmler set May 5 as the target date.

Louis Haefliger, a Swiss member of the International Red Cross, had heard about Mauthausen and its subcamps. On April 28, 1945, he had tried to bring food to the prisoners. The SS commander refused to let him deliver the packages. Haefliger returned two days later and tried again. This time he became friendly with an SS officer, who told him about Himmler's plan. Haefliger knew he had to stop Himmler, but how?

On May 4, Haefliger and his friend painted an SS car white with a red cross on the hood. This is the official emblem of the International Red Cross. Then they set out to find Allied troops and bring them back to rescue the prisoners before it was too late.

On the morning of May 5, a platoon of twenty-three American soldiers from the 11th Armored Division, led by Sergeant Al Kosiek, scouted the area near Mauthausen. "Suddenly one of our men stumbled onto some people who seemed to be in some large cages," recalled Kosiek. These were prisoners at Gusen III. Kosiek disarmed the forty German guards and sent them back to head-quarters escorted by two peeps (small jeeps). As Kosiek and his platoon moved on, they heard a vehicle approaching. It was Haefliger's red-cross car. Haefliger jumped out and told Kosiek about Mauthausen and its subcamps. He urged Kosiek to get there quickly before Himmler blew up the tunnels at Gusen I and II with the prisoners inside.

As Kosiek's platoon approached Gusen I and II, an SS captain who had remained came forward. Kosiek, with the help of one of his men who spoke German, explained that he was taking over the camp. The SS captain surrendered quietly.

Then Kosiek's platoon continued on its way to Mauthausen. The men stopped at the entrance to the camp, outside the electrified wire fence. "Behind that fence were hundreds of people who went wild with joy when they first sighted us," recalled Kosiek. "It's a sight I'll never forget." He and his men were stunned by what they saw. Dead bodies. Walking skeletons.

The prisoners were thrilled to see the Americans. Miraculously, Wiesenthal was still alive. "Those who could move at all staggered or crawled out of the shacks," he remembered. Thousands of starving men and women joyfully greeted the Americans. "Freedom!" they shouted in their many native languages—from Spanish, Italian, and French to Polish and Czech. "Liberty!"

"Some waved their own long-hidden national flags," recalled Chaplain Mark Geeslin of the 11th Armored Division.

But the prisoners who had made the secret gift did not bring it out yet. Perhaps they had not finished. Or they may have been waiting for the right person to give it to, and the right moment. The camp had broken down into chaos; Kosiek tried to maintain order as everyone went wild.

In the courtyard, Spanish prisoners threw a rope around the bronze German eagle mounted on top of the gate. They pulled until it came crashing down. Then they draped a long banner on the wall with a greeting painted in Spanish: LOS ESPAÑOLES ANTIFASCISTAS SALUDAN A LA FUERZAS LIBERADORAS (The Spanish Anti-Fascists welcome the liberating forces).

Lieutenant Jack Taylor introduced himself to Kosiek. He told Kosiek that there were two other American prisoners in the camp, Sergeant Louis Biagioni and Lionel Romney, an African-American fireman in the Merchant Marine. "The band then played 'The Star-Spangled Banner,'" remembered Kosiek, "and my emotions were so great that the song suddenly meant more to me than it ever did before. Many of the refugees were crying as they watched our platoon standing at attention, presenting arms."

Kosiek put Lieutenant Taylor, Sergeant Biagioni, and Lionel Romney into a jeep. Then he rounded up the one thousand Austrian guards and ordered them to load their weapons into the platoon's three trucks. After telling the freed prisoners to cooperate and stay calm, Kosiek promised to come back quickly with help. He and his twenty-two men marched the guards to headquarters. Along the way they picked up the guards at Gusen and took their weapons, too. Altogether Kosiek's platoon brought eighteen hundred German prisoners to headquarters by late that night. His commanding officer, Colonel Richard R. Seibel, could hardly believe his eyes.

The next morning, May 6, the Americans returned to Mauthausen under the command of Richard R. Seibel, who had just been promoted to colonel. Although some say that Colonel Seibel got out of his car and walked into Mauthausen, Přem Dobiáš remembered it differently. According to Dobiáš, Colonel Seibel rolled into Mauthausen in a tank. "He opened the turret and took off his goggles. Everything was quiet." Then Colonel Seibel saluted the more than twelve thousand survivors gathered before him as though they were fellow soldiers. The people cheered.

Now the group who had made the special gift stepped forward. They were crying as they unfurled it and gave it to Colonel Seibel. It was a big American flag, more than six feet long—large enough to fly from a flagpole. "Colonel Seibel took the flag, lifted it up, and kissed it," remembered Přem Dobiáš.

"I thanked them and thanked them," said Colonel Seibel.

As he examined the flag he noticed something. There were thirteen red and ivory white stripes, which stood for the original thirteen colonies. But instead of forty-eight stars representing each state of the union at that time, there were fifty-six. The prisoners had guessed how many states there were in America. They had added an extra row.

Their gift deeply moved Colonel Seibel. He realized what incredible spirit and courage it had taken for them to make it. He understood that the flag symbolized liberty and the promise of a better life.

That very day Colonel Seibel ran up the Stars and Stripes on the flagpole—with all fifty-six stars. The handmade American flag flew over the camp that was now free.

"I couldn't believe it," said Mike Jacobs. "Were we actually free? I had waited so long to hear that beautiful song, the beautiful music, those beautiful words that I was free."

As for Himmler, he lost all power and prestige during the final weeks of the war. The Nazis themselves, as well as the Allies, sought his arrest. He was captured by the British on May 21. Before he could be brought to trial, he swallowed poison and died. Thus, Himmler was defeated. Approximately half of the two hundred thousand people he had imprisoned at Mauthausen and made to suffer so terribly left there alive.

The flag made by the Mauthausen prisoners is now in the Simon Wiesenthal Center in Los Angeles, California.

AFTERWORD

Some people say that a few women prisoners made the flag with fifty-six stars, while others say it was mostly men. The exact identities of those who made it may never be known. Many details about the liberation of the concentration camp at Mauthausen remain in question. Scholars and historians continue to study records and eye-witness accounts. Today the flag is displayed in the Simon Wiesenthal Center's Museum of Tolerance in Los Angeles, California. Peter Seibel donated it in honor of his father, Colonel Richard Seibel, and as a tribute to Simon Wiesenthal.

For Wiesenthal, the stars of the American flag took on a special meaning. "One was the star of hope, one that of justice, of tolerance, of friendship, of brotherly love, of understanding," he said. "In the stripes I saw the roads to freedom."

Wiesenthal regarded the American flag as "a symbol of our liberation, for which I will always be grateful, and of the promise that we would be able to go on living as free men."

He gave Colonel Seibel credit for restoring not only his health, but his sense of dignity as a human being. Colonel Seibel stayed at Mauthausen for thirty-five days with his troops and cared for the emaciated prisoners. He gave them oat bread, nourishing soup, vegetables, and medicine. Through his efforts, countless lives were saved.

After liberation, Wiesenthal settled in Austria, first in Linz and then in Vienna. However, he decided not to go back to his profession as an architect. Instead, he devoted his life to bringing Nazi war criminals to justice.

The Simon Wiesenthal Center, founded in 1977, is an international center for Holocaust remembrance and the defense of human rights and the Jewish people. Headquartered in Los Angeles, California, and named for Simon Wiesenthal, the center, museum, library, and archives are a multimedia resource for education and research.

The government of Austria preserved the main camp at Mauthausen as a place of remembrance and learning. The Mauthausen Memorial includes a museum, library, and archives, open every day of the week. Thousands of people visit each year. They walk down 186 steps to the bottom of the quarry, a lasting reminder of the evils of Mauthausen.

REFERENCES

An asterisk (*) indicates works suitable for young readers.

Publications

Barlev, Zvi. *Would God It Were Night.* New York: Vantage Press, 1991.

Bridgman, Jon. *The End of the Holocaust: The Liberation of the Camps.* Portland, Oreg.: Areopagitica Press, 1990.

*Crampton, William. *Flag.* New York: Alfred A. Knopf, Eyewitness Books, 1989.

*Crouthers, David D. *Flags of American History.* Maplewood, N.J.: C. S. Hammond & Company, 1962.

**Frommer's Austria.* New York: Macmillan Travel USA, 1999.

"G.I.'s Remember: Liberating the Concentration Camps." National Museum of American Jewish Military History (July 1994): 52–75.

*Gilman, Susan. "Mauthausen: Youthful Encounter with Absolute Evil." *The Jewish Week* (May 26, 1989): 29.

Horwitz, Gordon J. *Shadow of Death: Living Outside the Gates of Mauthausen.* New York: The Free Press, 1990.

*Jacobs, Mike. *Holocaust Survivor.* Austin, Tex.: Eakin Press, 2001.

*Kosiek, Staff Sgt. Albert J. "Liberation of Mauthausen (and Gusen I, II & III)." *The Thunderbolt* 8, no. 7 (May–June 1955): unpaged.

Le Chêne, Evelyn. *Mauthausen: The History of a Death Camp.* London: Methuen & Co., Ltd., 1971.

Levitt, Peter. "The Fires Within." *Los Angeles Times Magazine* (January 9, 1994): 16–17, 20–21, 32.

Liberating the Concentration Camps. Washington, D.C.: National Museum of American Jewish Military History, 1994.

**The Liberators.* Los Angeles: Simon Wiesenthal Center, 1985.

Manvell, Roger, and Heinrich Fraenkel. *Himmler.* New York: G. P. Putnam's Sons, 1965.

Padfield, Peter. *Himmler.* New York: Henry Holt and Company, 1990.

*Parrish, Thomas. *The American Flag.* New York: Simon & Schuster, 1973.

Pick, Hela. *Simon Wiesenthal: A Life in Search of Justice.* Boston: Northeastern University Press, 1996.

Pike, David Wingeate. *Spaniards in the Holocaust: Mauthausen, the Horror on the Danube.* London and New York: Routledge, 2000.

*Rogasky, Barbara. *Smoke and Ashes: The Story of the Holocaust.* 2nd ed. revised and expanded. New York: Holiday House, 2002.

*Rollo, Vera. *The American Flag.* Lanham, Md.: The Maryland Historical Press, 1991.

Rozett, Robert, and Shmuel Spector. *Encyclopedia of the Holocaust.* Jerusalem: Yad Vashem; New York: Facts on File, 2000.

Shirer, William L. *The Rise and Fall of the Third Reich.* New York: Simon & Schuster, 1960.

Storm, Ralph. "Mail Call." *The Thunderbolt* 51, no. 2 (April 1997): unpaged.

Wiesenthal, Simon. *The Murderers Among Us.* London: Heinemann, 1967.

———. Speech delivered upon being awarded the U.S. Congressional Medal of Honor by President Jimmy Carter, May 8, 1980.